The Land
of Milk and Honey

WITHDRAWN

Publication of this book was supported by a grant from the
Eric Mathieu King Fund of The Academy of American Poets.

THE
James
DICKEY
CONTEMPORARY POETRY SERIES

EDITED BY RICHARD HOWARD

The Land
of
Milk and Honey

Poems by
Sarah Getty

UNIVERSITY OF SOUTH CAROLINA PRESS

Published in Columbia, South Carolina, by the
University of South Carolina Press

Manufactured in the United States of America

00 99 98 97 96   5 4 3 2 1

Library of Congress Cataloging-in-Publication Data

Getty, Sarah, 1943–
   The land of milk and honey : poems / by Sarah Getty.
      p.   cm. — (The James Dickey contemporary poetry series)
   ISBN 1–57003–158–4 (cloth). — ISBN 1–57003–159–2 (paper)
   I. Title. II. Series.
PS3557.E885L36 1996
811'.54—dc20   96–25250

for my mother, Davina Ely Sovereign,

and

for David and Lisa

Contents

A Note on Sarah Getty

None of the obstacles, the problems, the bafflements which poetry presents, these days, to the Common Reader (who of course may not, these days, exist at all—and to the Uncommon Reader poetry presents no more than a request for attention, a claim on the time otherwise allotted to science, or to history, or even to the domestic economy) is to be found in this collection with which Sarah Getty begins her life as a poet.

Neither the disjunctive shades of Jorie Graham nor the daunting intimacies of Sharon Olds (to stay with the women, merely) are operative here, to any degree. If there is a mentorial figure behind the ease and entertainment which these well-made, worked-out poems afford, it is not so likely to be a poet at all (though Mona Van Duyn does float to the surface of association) but rather a chef or a shrink such as Julia Child or Anna Freud (to stay with the women, merely).

Getty makes no trouble: she wants us to get into her poems, to get through them, and to get out of them with a minimum of fuss; her emblem of duration might well be the effective recipe, the revelatory psychonalytic session. Just look at her poems on the page—carefully counted out, the stanzas leaving plenty of room to breathe, the long lines promising that all will be confided, in due time. Just listen to her sensible music:

> . . . The Only Child leans back
> into my arms and I lean
> back into my mother's, home again. Rocking
> we watch the west for omens unfolding in the gold.

The varied enjambment of *back* and the long O's of *Only* and *home* and *omen* sealed with the rhyming O's of *unfolding* and *gold* are sufficient to inscribe the lines in the aural memory, to finish, as Julia Child would say, with a demiglaze. Sarah Getty doesn't go in for more spectacular effects, she wants neither to intimidate nor to dazzle, but her poems always function at a level just above the tension of the lyre, as Wallace Stevens called it, where the language has its way with us, even while we are having ours with it. Such is the plain style, its eminent dignity and its secret design.

Of course some notice might be taken—this is where Anna Freud comes in, I guess—of the interesting commitment this poet has made to the gynaeceum; her poems are all "about" that wonderful concatenation of experience which moves from mother down to maiden, from maiden back up to mother, by way of the married daughter—Getty is good at all the parts, she does the female in different voices—without much attention given, or even loaned, to the father, the husband, the son. If love is blind, marriage restores its sight with remarkable acuteness in these poems, and I believe we are in the presence of a new, a post-feminism here, an attitude which is neither militant nor resentful, but remarkably exploratory and resilient. As Ivy Compton-Burnett reminds us, and Sarah Getty exemplifies, there is more difference within the sexes than between them (see "Pocket Guide" in what follows).

But if she is personal (always a good idea when you are talking about a person), this poet is never private; and if she is heterogeneous (always a good idea when you are talking about a gender), this poet is never public: she is identical, and her poems are the elated statements of that self which delights to be conscious of its duties. A poet is someone who has invented a poet; I am happy to welcome Sarah Getty's invention, her identity on the pages of our attention. Chesterton said it was unwise in the poet to goad the sleeping lion of laughter. On the contrary, it seems to me, in Getty's poems, that the highest wisdom, and the truest value, is to be found in the presence of her waking lion on almost every page—or is it lioness?

Richard Howard

Acknowledgments

The author wishes to thank Richard Howard for his help with these poems. Grateful acknowledgment is made to these publications, in which the following poems have previously appeared:

The Beloit Poetry Journal
  "Cleaning the Storm Windows"
The New Republic:
  "Getting Clearer"
  "Presbyopia"
The Paris Review
  "Corn"
  "Mother May I"
  "The Wash"
Shenandoah
  "After a Quarrel"
  "The Oseberg Ship"
  "sit. anx. reg. fert."
  "Troupers"
  "Music Cruise"
  "Thanksgiving"
Western Humanities Review
  "Deer, 6:00 A.M."
  "Channel 2: Horowitz Playing Mozart"

*The Land
of Milk and Honey*

I

That Woman

The Wash

A round white troll with a black, greasy
heart shuddered and hummed "Diogenes,
Diogenes," while it sloshed the wash.
It stayed in the basement, a cave-dank
place I could only like on Mondays,
helping Mother. My job was stirring
the rinse. The troll hummed. Its wringer stuck
out each piece of laundry like a tongue—

socks, aprons, Daddy's shirts, my brother's
funny (I see London) underpants.
The whole family came past, mashed flat
as Bugs Bunny pancaked by a train.
They flopped into the rinse tub and learned
to swim, relaxing, almost arms and legs
again. I helped the transformation
with a stick we picked up one summer

at the lake. Wave-peeled, worn to gray, inch
thick, it was a first rate stirring stick.
Apprenticed on my stool, I sang a rhyme
of Simple Simon gone afishing
and poked the clothes around the cauldron
and around. The wringer was risky.
Touch it with just your fingertip,
it would pull you in and spit you out

flat as a dishrag. It grabbed Mother
once—rolled her arm right to the elbow.
But she kept her head, flipped the lever
to reverse, and got her arm back, pretty
and round as new. This was a story
from Before. Still, I seemed to see it—
my mother brave as a movie star,
the flattened arm pumping up again,

like Popeye's. I fished out the rinsing
swimmers, one by one. Mother fed them
back to the wringer and they flopped, flat,
into baskets. Then the machine peed
right on the floor; the foamy water
curled around the drain and gurgled down.
Mother, under the slanting basement
doors, where it was darkest, reached up that

miraculous arm and raised the lid.
Sunlight fell down the stairs, shouting
"This way out!" There was the day, an Easter
egg cut-out of grass and trees and sky.
Mother lugged the baskets up. Too short
to reach the clothesline, I would slide down
the bulkhead or sit and drum my heels
to aggravate the troll (Who's that trit-

trotting . . .) and watch. Thus I learned the rules
of hanging clothes: Shirts went upside down,
pinned at the placket and seams. Sheets hung
like hammocks; socks were a toe-bitten
row. Underpants, indecently mixed,
flapped chainwise, cheek to cheek. Mother
took hold of the clothespole like a knight
couching his lance and propped the sagging

4

line up high, to catch the wind. We all
were airborne then, sleeves puffed out round
as sausages, bottoms billowing,
legs in arabesque. Our heaviness
was scattered into air, our secrets
bleached back to white. Mother stood easing
her back and smiled, queen of the backyard
and all that flapping crowd. For a week

now, each day, we'd put on this jubilee,
walk inside it, wash with it, and sleep
in its sweetness. At night, best of all,
I'd see with closed eyes the sheets aloft,
pajamas dancing, pillow cases
shaking out white signals in the sun,
and my mother with the basket, bent
and then rising, stretching up her arms.

Mother, May I?

During the screened-porch dinner of corn on the cob,
pork chops, tomatoes like red meat, warm and bleeding,
I felt the first stirring. The air moved, cracked the damp
heat that stood around the house in blocks. The backyard

maple rustled, twenty thousand green hands waving
a signal. Robins up and down the block began
scattering their coded notes. Our yard stretched larger
as the sky lost light. Out by the lilac hedge,

imaginary shapes conspired. I had to scrape
scraps into the kitchen can, rinse and stack the plates,
while outside, I knew it, everything was starting
without me. On the porch, the kittens, one tiger,

one marmalade, were climbing right up the screens
to chase the white moths that bumped on the other side,
dying, like dumbbells, to enter our box of light.
I stood on the sill, where tomatoes were lined up

to ripen, and unhooked the tiger from the screen.
Under the fur my fingers felt her secret, hot,
skinny body; her heart like a tom-tom hammered.
Then I heard Roger calling down the block, and John

did that whistle with his fingers. The dishes clinked
in the pan. Better not ask. Just, carefully,
open the porch door a crack, so the kittens won't
escape from safety, and slide out, like gliding

into warm, easy water. I ran on the grass,
I was gone. The air had a secret, sweetened
and heavy, like Hawaii, like honeymoons. Kids
were lined up already, across a yard where no

father was watering, solemnly wig-wagging
his hose. "Red Rover" was first. Whoever got named
had to charge like a ram into the other line,
try to break their phalanx of linked arms. Over

and over we flung ourselves, crashed and bounced and broke.
Later came "Mother, May I?" and then "Statues": grab
somebody's arm and whirl him around and around
and let go! He must freeze in whatever funny

pose he's flung into—Frankenstein, ballet dancer,
airplane, ape. Our bodies amazed us, taking shapes,
by chance, stranger than we could plan. Then, suddenly—
"Not It!" "Not It!" "Not It!"—we switched to Hide and Seek.

It was real night now, moon blue and humid. Mothers
would be calling soon. I hid in the hydrangea;
John was It. Lightning bugs rose in constellations
and sank, and rose again, blinking their welcomes. Sweat

prickled my neck, my scraped knee bled. I was hidden,
but anyway my heart beat hard. I was holding it,
secret, like a lightning bug cupped in my hand.
I was letting it rise in rhythm with its kind.

Corn

Our forest, our ocean, it stretched westward from the edge
of town. Knee high at fireworks time, taller by August
than any child. Flat as a bed the prairie, spread quilt
after quilt with green and tufted rows. Leaves waved in wind
like streamers, hung like ruffles. Each ear had its tassle—

gold silk hung down like the hair of a mother leaning
at dinnertime over the steaming stove. But really
the leaves had cutting edges, the stems were stiff, the rows
marched in regiments out to the Rockies, marched to feed
and keep us, like fathers marching against Germany,

away in rows and home again in rows. Away, and home
again, my father drove each day. Not to war, to work
at the corn plant. Not the green kind—the gray, conveyer-
belted buildings, asphalt, warehouse, a dim sun warming
the gray, stinking haze that was the only weather there.

The smell filled every inch of air, pocket or drawer, eyes,
hair. The price of alchemy—boxcars of gold disgorged
at the siding, cracked, soaked, fermented, milled, baked, transformed
to automated streams—liquid, powder, yellow, white,
clear as water. Masked girls in Bottling watched for flaws

as glass battalions paraded beneath the spouts. Gold
was Mazola, clear Karo—names of our household gods.
Argo, too, the white starch boxed in blue, the Indian
Maiden on the front. Her body was a slender ear
of corn; her look was proud and she held, it seems to me,

a spear. Better far than the girl on the salt box, queen
of Illinois at least, she was a friend whose riches
came home to us in Daddy's pockets. Some August days
he'd stop at a roadside stand, bring home a dozen green
ears in a brown bag. (Always he carried that bad smell

of work; it hung in his clothes like a curse.) Ears the shape
of generation, lapped in tough green wrappings. I knelt
and braced them between my knees, struggled to unswaddle
those mysteries. My brother, his biceps like baseballs,
could strip an ear in three pulls. Bared, the tender rows
   glowed

like pearls, translucent, taut to the touch. Inside each bump
the treasured wetness, soon to be steaming, sweet. Sneaking,
we would steal a tooth-touch just at the tip. Then we picked
from our sweat-damp arms the golden hairs of silk that stuck
there, signs, Mother said, of kids growing into corn folk,

sheathed in green and bodies all rows of bumps. One summer
we grew our own, in a garden plot down by the tracks.
You needed two rows, at least, to let the pollen waft
from male to female—those things the teacher talked about
in science. We liked it more than we would ever say,

weeding between the carrots and the beans those drawn out
summer evenings. The sky glowed gold-rose above a row
of poplars where a robin kept shaking out its scroll.
Our parents watered and hoed, now tall as the tasselled
corn, now bent to their tools like peasants. Handling

that clean-smelling dirt that felt like crumbs of silk, we slapped
happily at mosquitoes and left tribal markings
mixed of blood, sweat, and earth. Daddy, stopping for a smoke,
looked like a handsome soldier in his khakis. Mother,
our gypsy, knew the robin's language. Something older,

bigger, and kind was working there, like a huge plow horse
gentle in its harness. Even the riotous beans
stayed in their rows and behaved around their stakes. Beyond
the garden plots a train might hoot and pass, streaming west-
ward like a straightened silver snake. We would stand and wave

a carrot or an ear of corn at diners gliding
right out of Illinois. We were not even dreaming
yet of states where land could rise in rocks and not repeat
those uniform green rows. We had our whole lives right there
in the palms of our hands. Our maps were lines drawn through
    corn.

The Oseberg Ship

To take in the shape of it—
whale, kraken, wing, fish, myth—fleet, almost
black in the bright hall, the white vault hollowed
just to fit; to stand where the strakes converge, breast
air, rear, and spout that prow higher
than icons in books conveyed—

mighty swan, sea horse, seventh
wave recurving, cresting in tendril
curl, world-admired spiral carried so long in mind;
to touch, when the guard's not looking, the dark wood,
color of earth, the carved web edging
the curve, interlace flowing

as seaweed, focussed as snowflakes—
this to me is mana, pilgrimage,
but even a whisper, to share it, is too
heated for your cool youth. A head-shake throws off
my attempt to catch you in that net
of fingered-over facts

and longings we old ones trail
everywhere with us. You hush me, frown
down at a placard: The ship was old, long past
its travels in the gannet's bath. On its deck
they built a wooden tent and laid there
a pair of passengers.

Whatever the two might need
was put aboard—tapestries, apples,
pots—then the ship was sunk on the spot in earth.
Long time they were meant to journey together,
those two dead. And not all easy sailing,
either. A dozen horses

were stabled in the grave;
a cart and three sledges were ready
to carry the pair if the watery way
gave out. Battlemates, were they? Chief and thane?
Or traders, racers of the whale road,
braving the sea's white teeth?

No—for the find "lacks weapons"
and includes "a wealth of objects
connected with the work of women." Two female
skeletons were found. One, they say, was fifty.
Her bones and shoes complain of swollen,
arthritic feet. The other

is a puzzle of younger
bones, young enough to be the old one's
daughter. Daughter, even you are caught now.
You have heard of offspring taken into death
to fetch and carry. I have heard
of daughters who so burned

with love they left off living.
Or—so reads a third surmise—the two
died at once of the same plague or fever.
You turn to me, complaining. We put our heads
and guesses together. We seem to need
to know: did the young one struggle,

recalcitrant to the last
blade-bite? Or did she use the knife
herself, cutting carefully, not severing
the tie? Or did the two lie side by side
in fever's fire, hot hands clasping
until their grasp gave way?

One of these stories (like it
or not) is true. We feel its power
now—how it bends the strakes to their boatshape
and lifts the prow. We see how ancient patterns
rise and twine, like the buried Serpent
stirring, occulting the bright hall.

Alive, blind and unkind as Fate,
they embrace us, braid us into their lace:
monster and prey, victim and victim, enemy
interlocked with enemy. You eye me,
blank and cagey as the day you came.
When the salvage team broke

the barrow, hauled up this wreck,
sifted the manmade fragments from the earth,
and pieced with male precision the jigsaw find
together, they should have left below in the cleft
mound the female things—spindle, silk, comb,
bones and crippled slippers

and twining lives. In earth,
in darkness, in time they might have ripened
safely, in safety (almost) fed us secretly.
Let them descend; let them get on with their journey.
And we two, stuck for the moment eye
to eye, will turn and get on

with ours. What we came so far
to see was this: the empty ship,
the glide and flight of it, the virile prow,
the narrow, abstract shape that rides so lightly
in the high, the bright, the carefully
hollowed chambers of the mind.

Pocket Guide

You dropped out of my pocket.
"This one's got a pocket, too,"
they said—it was the first thing

anybody noticed.
Wrinkled, empty, not even
a penny in it for luck,

it's all I issued you, gear
for your stay here. By this time
you're figuring what it's for;

you've fingered it, found it's made
of damp silk and sea smell, shaped
like secrets. Bald as a fig

once, lately it's got a fringe—
a sign that you're fit to get
this further information:

It is not for carrying
money, lipstick or keys, though
there's no harm in trying, and

it does expand, like a mesh
purse, or a concertina.
Too, it can make a wheezy

music, or pulse a rhythm,
drumhead to a gifted stick.
It can mimic other wet

accessories—throb like a heart,
hanker like a stomach, dream
and decide things like a brain.

You will find rules—lists of them,
all different—telling what may
or may not be put inside,

by whom, when, where, how and why.
These are best disregarded,
especially mine. It's your

pocket, keep it clean or dirty,
stuff it with candy or trash,
bead it, braid it, blow dry it,

dye it blue, tattoo it, wash
and wear it on your sleeve, lend
it, rent it, time-share with option

to buy—or better yet, take it
on the road. "The Amazing,
Musical, Magic Pocket!"

Pull out flags, rabbits, flowers,
fruit, flutes, balloons. It's an act
that lays them in the aisles.

Don't be surprised if the sleight
gets out of hand and you grab
forth goodies unlooked for: gold

doubloons, ivory, myrrh.
Keep it coming, keep your skills
up, and if your timing's right

you might get down to the prize
that's hiding at the bottom
of the pocket—a Kewpie

doll, damp silk, with a wrinkled,
empty pocket and a mouth
full of loud complaints. Fill it,

feed the mouth, fill up the head
with truth. Say, "This is your own
pocket. With reasonable

care, it will give many years
of pleasure. Find its surprises.
Play with it. Pass it on."

sit. anx. reg. fert.

Calm as a blue pill (ten milligrams
of Valium) I'm enthroned,
though flat on my back and helpless as
a pasha. My heavy limbs
are regally disposed—legs spread and
hung up on racks like pasta,
one arm cuffed and laid out on a sort
of tray, the other feeling
the IV's vampire bite. I'm gracious.
Grandly, I greet my nurses,
Betty and Fran. They're here to witness

my lying in this state—awake, to
boot—through everything that's next.
Bill, the anesthesiologist,
stands by, like a priest, to be
called in at need. My heart is blipping
greenly on his screen. My heart
is perfect. Nothing's wrong with me. But
Blue Cross won't cough up without
a diagnosis. I didn't know what it was, until I peeked
at my chart in Pre-Op. "sit. anx. reg.

fert." A puzzle to pass the time with.
Well, there's only one "anx." these
days—anxiety, our reigning boogey
queen. But what's "sit. anx?" Sit . . . sit . . .
Memory murmurs a phrase I read

in *Newsweek,* something like a
TV comedy. —Situational!
So that's what I've got: "situ-
ational anxiety." Then "reg.
fert." must mean I suffer from
"situational anxiety

regarding fertility." What a
whiz that doctor is, to find
such a fancy sickness in my soul,
with no more said (and that by
him) than, "At your age, if you don't have
your tubes tied soon, you won't get
your money's worth." Macbeth, take heed—they
can minister to a mind
diseased. Granted, my situation's
less than your lady's, but *my*
anxiety will be surgically

removed! The doctor washes his hands,
obsessively, then stands between
my legs to scrub what he calls my "tum-
my." (He is called "Doctor," what
else?) It tickles. I'm feeling no pain
until he shoves in a rod
to push my womb around. (Any sass,
and it could be next to go.)
At last he withdraws from my acute
angle, stands at my side like
a man at a salad bar. Needles,

novocain, the cut in the belly
button—easiest entrance,
old mouth puckered shut since it stopped sucking
on my mother. Next they blow

up my belly with gas; it burgeons,
nostalgic for brooding. We
laugh—it's hysterical! The table
tilts me back. My intestines
slither from harm's way, cuddle up to
my lungs. Novocain to the
tubes. Then, it seems, large hardware—crowbars,

plumber's helpers—is jamming my gut.
Blessed Bill administers
his unction, "A little short-acting
narcotic." Ah—I sink into
a circle of light, in a circle
of darkness. The table rocks
back with me, then up, then back again,
as if tossing on water.
I am dipped down twice, three times, in the
name of the father and of
the mother and of the only child.

I gasp in a deep full of monsters
and little boys never born.
Bright souls wave like anemones, barred
from my body forever.
Below them I can see the Old Ones—
the Sick King, the Trickster, the
Witch, the Priestess, the Thief. The Lost Child
is there, and the Bad Mother.
Immortal, gestating in the brain's
moist folds, they queue up by the
exit. "The first one's done." I surface.

Everything's plain again. The second
one's a snap. "Want to take a
look?" The doctor swivels the eyepiece,

and I contemplate myself
through my navel, with a straw stuck into
the soda of my vitals.
That slick red hump is the uterus,
surfacing like a mara-
schino whale. There is an ovary,
pale as marshmallow cream. There
is a tube, pinker than a bride's thigh

in its tight white garter. There is the
other one, collared, clerical.
"I take thee to be my wedded life,"
I vow. A future flows through
these tubes now, blocked as they are: poems,
novels, travel, time. I swell
with it, fecund and greedy, until
they pull out their tools. The doctor
stiches, snips, deft as Fate. Thanking Bill
and Fran, I am delivered,
at last, to the Surgical Day Care

Unit. Wheeling me, nurse Betty looms
by my perambulator,
coos at me, and tucks in my blanket.
I am the fair-haired girl now,
anxiety gone, like a headache
in a TV ad. They praise
my bright eyes, my appetite. They bring
me a chicken sandwich and a
Fresca, but it's too late. Cut loose and
hungry, I have already
eaten the afterbirth, cord and all.

That Woman

Look! A flash of orange along the river's edge—
"oriole!" comes to your lips like instinct, then
it's vanished—lost in the foliage,

in all your head holds, getting on with the day.
But not gone for good. There is that woman
walks unseen beside you with her apron

pockets full. Days later, or years, when you least
seem to need it—reading Frost on the subway,
singing over a candled cake—she'll reach

into a pocket and hand you this intact
moment—the river, the orange streak parting
the willow, and the "oriole!" that leapt

to your lips. Unnoticed, steadfast, she gathers
all this jumble, sorts it, hands it back like
prizes from Cracker Jack. She is your mother,

who first said, "Look! a robin!" and pointed
and there was a robin, because her own
mother had said to her, "Look!" and pointed,

and so on, back to the beginning: the mother,
the child, and the world. The damp bottom
on one arm and pointing with the other:

the peach tree, the small rocks in the shallows,
the moon and the man in the moon. So you keep on,
seeing, forgetting, faithfully followed;

and you yourself, unwitting, gaining weight,
have thinned to invisibility, become
that follower. Even now, your daughter

doesn't see you at her elbow as she walks
the beach. There! a gull dips to the Pacific,
and she points and says to the baby, "Look!"

II

Notes from Noah's Boat

Troupers

Two rings away, the gorillas are waltzing
in pairs. Soon the lady gorillas
will take off their heads and step

out of their hairy cocoons—they are really
glittering women who climb right up
to the top of those ropes

and dance there, pointing and spinning like weather-
cocks, while down on the sawdust the male
gorillas man, or ape, the ropes.

In the center ring, the lion tamer snaps
the big she-cats into orbit. They
ring his small, dense center, faster

than planets, wilder than electrons. Later,
he will seek glory in the black hole
of the lioness's mouth.

In the meantime, the clowns clown around, fifteen
elephants lean in a pyramid,
and the watching faces, like

rows of scribbled o's, open and close around
noises and cotton candy. People
drift out to the bathrooms or

snackbars, come back with popcorn, get to know their
neighbors, smack their kids. Like tourists in
a cathedral, or the Grand

Canyon, they're numbed by the splendor, too little
to take it all in. Even the spot-
lights, meant to help, confuse them.

Luckily, we are not in charge of all this.
We're only two-ninths of a small act
in the third ring, called Wanda's

Canine Wonders. Tonight, you are inside our
little keg, running hard, rolling it
clockwise around the ring.

I am on top, outside the keg, facing backward,
my feet busy as a lumberjack's,
letting it roll beneath me.

Tomorrow night, I will be inside, rolling
the keg, and you will be outside it,
running the other way. But

the keg will roll just as it always does, no
matter who's inside. And no matter
what we do, nobody much

will watch us, what with the rope-dancing ladies,
the lions, the elephants, and the
other dogs riding their bikes.

But that is not our concern. We have only
to roll our little keg clockwise
around the ring, inside and

outside, on alternating nights. Nobody else
does it better, and it's not exactly
easy. The one inside works

harder, but the one on top might fall off, so
it evens out. We make progress, though
once the circle is complete

we just have to go around again. It's not
what we had in mind when we first joined
the circus, but it's our own

specialty now, and like Wanda always says,
"In this business, if you get a good act
together, don't mess with it."

Cleaning the Storm Windows

They look like idiots,
or the meeting of space aliens,
gesturing in palm-out circles
flat on the air between them.
They crouch, bend nearer, squint,
pointing, directing each other,

"There, no—over there—a smear."
"No, that's on your side."
All but nose-to-nose, they never touch.
She grimaces, rubs. "Sorry,
but I can see that it's on your side,
Honey." He brings a work-lamp nearer.

They look and wince.
"It's a mess all over;
we'll have to start again."
In the bright light they
squirt and rub, stand and squat
like off-beat mirror twins

or actors botching a bit of mime.
"Jesus, let's quit," she says.
He says he guesses it'll do.
They maneuver the empty square
out of the garage, ludicrous
and careful as a vaudeville skit.

She says, "Mr. Bones, it 'pears to me
that your side still could use some work."

Deer, 6:00 A.M.

The deer—neck not birch trunk, eyes
not leaf or shadow, comes clear
from nowhere at the eye's edge.
The woman's legs stop. Her mind
lags, then flashes, "Deer at edge
of the woods." The deer's eyes, black
and fragile, stare back and stop

her breathing. The breeze drops. Light
shines every leaf. She enters
that other world, her feet stone
still on the path. The deer stands
pat and takes her in. Antlered,
static as an animal—
not a statue, photograph,

any substitute—can be
because it wants to, it includes
her in the world it watches.
She notes its coat, thick, stiff
like straw, with a straw-like shine.
There, where the ribs are, she sees
no rise or fall of breathing.

She breathes, shyly, attempting
the etiquette of quiet.
She goes over what she knows
of antlers, those little trees

of bone, grown for a season
and shed like leaves. The deer's head,
she thinks, is hieroglyphic,

eyes of wet ink, unblinking.
No golden links clasp the neck—
no deer of Arthur's this, sent
as a sign. The woman finds
and fingers these few deer-thoughts
in her mind. But she's no match
for its stasis, she hasn't

the tact. Tableau, entrancement—
but what's the second panel
of the tapestry? She moves,
not back, discreetly, as one
would leave a king, but forward,
to have it done. To free (or,
less likely, fall on one knee,

petitioning). The deer moves,
smooth as a fish, is gone. Green
edges waver and reknit.
The light shifts. The woman, two-
legged still, walks on. "I saw
a deer," she will say, pouring
coffee. Not "I was." "I saw."

Crows, Whales

I.

Mornings, when you're still in the gray deep,
dreaming a drowned treasure, a tender

fish-man, pleasure's in rising slowly
to the lighter layers, while forests

of red coral sink, grow indistinct
like Polaroid pictures in reverse.

But the sharp beaks of crows break open
the outer gray and fire their barbed yells

deep into your sleep. They want to tweak you
from your mystery and hang you up

dripping on the sky. You slip the hook,
roll, and dive. Too late—you're yanked awake

enough to know that crows don't holler
their black alarms to you. Eavesdropper

merely, accidental catch, you're thrown
back, floating, neither in deep nor aloft.

Outside, the crows go on debating—
or agreeing, who knows?—in urgent

chorus. From time to time you'd see one,
if you looked, crossing the window square,

scrawling its indecipherable
script onto the gray sheet of morning.

II.

On this blank page of the Atlantic,
parts of whales are written and erased.
Black triangles and bulges—flukes, fins,

wings (it seems), and noses appear, then
vanish. They rise up like memories
of dreams, jigsaw fragments that fade out

into gray. The young man who's paid to
"interpret" the whales tells us it's noise
that hooks them. We bang on the boat's sides,

stamp and holler to bring them nearer.
They circle us, bigger than buses.
Some do "spy hops," nosing up until

the eye emerges to observe us,
as it were, in our element. There—
one breaches, hangs in the air flinging

spiraled ropes of drops. We try to snap
the shutter at the peak—to catch one
in flight and keep it, if the timing's

right. If not, we'll carry home empty
frames of gray. But the film case, fumbled,
drops overboard, a vanishing black

pellet. Clammed up, keeping its secrets,
it will steep in the salt solution
and await developments—a starfish,

a riptide, or Judgment Day—to bring
its twelve hidden images to light.
Meanwhile, the whales' vaudeville goes on;

one lies on its back and flaps, others
hop and leap. The Interpreter says
"No one knows what this behavior means."

Filmless, with only our gray matter
to rely on, we watch and applaud.
We stamp our cold feet and yell for more.

You have been given—

not far from the house you keep, the yard
you must feed and water—
this water to feed on, to idle by.

You hunker on rock that slants
into the shallows and you wait there,
aspiring as a frog

struck dumb by sun. Here there are blueberries,
bunched like the ten breasts of some
old goddess; in each bunch each ripening

color—green, yellow, pink, mauve,
purple. Three within reach are blue enough
to eat, but you wait: you're caught

by the lighter blue of the little waves
rippling towards you. They lap
and break at your feet, where old foam, trapped

by a washed-up lily stem,
turns slowly brown. They lap and break endlessly,
pushed by the breeze that stiffens

in your face. Insistent, the bright wind rucks
the water up, puckering
the ridges with dimples of dark and sparkle

that sweep past in patches
like the patterns of wind on a wheatfield.
Insistent, the little waves

repeat on the rocks the same low, musical
"bloop." There's less mystery here
than you expected. It's clear that you should sit

and wait until the wind has thinned
you out, and the waves, that now must stop
at the water's edge, come loose

from the water and flow right through you,
weightless, invisible,
overlapping these older, frozen waves,

this gray-and-white grained rock.
Off shore, the water lilies, white and stiff
as the Egyptian lotus,

dip and rise to the waves' beat like ladies
in an exercise class.
In a gust their leaf-discs lift at one edge

and flap (their undersides
a rich, surprising red), as if a flock
of water lilies could take flight,

snapping their long tethers. The shadow
of the blueberry bush holds still
under water, on the sloping rock,

but the surface of the pond
ripples on and on and seems to shake
the shadow, rock and all.

The pond is netted with white sky light,
netted with green reflections
of the blueberry branches, and the rock

in the shallows, with its black
shadow of the bush, is crossed by a net
of moving yellow light

refracted from the wave-tops. The wind
and the little waves insist
that all manner of thing—the Fritos bag,

the beer can, the passing cars,
the red-and-white plastic bobber—will be well-
worn in time, in time will be smoothed

and quiet. Beside the bright net that sweeps
the pond, the gold net that rocks
in the shallows, you wait like a frog, or like

the tactful fish that always
matches the pitch of its surroundings—
to be taken, to be hauled in.

After a Quarrel: The Juilliard String Quartet

While the four men on the stage
sweat in their amazing labor,
mesh like cogs, lever their elbows,
twist and bow their bodies
to lift, lift the quartet like
a cube of marble they must
raise and balance on one corner,

I sit at a distance, too far
gone to hear them. I am rehearsing
the same mistake, over and over,
getting it perfectly wrong.

The music is showing that old
man how to do it: stepping from
one note to the next note and
the next, attentive, secure.
"On Friday, lunch, then a nap,
then the Juilliard." Small joys in
firm series, lengthening his days.

I go from one word to the next
word and back again. I foul my
footprints, muddy the breadcrumbs
I dropped the last time around.

That woman is leaning her head
back, as if soaking in the tub.

She lies slain by beauty, like
the Lily Maid, transported
downstream to somewhere I should
remember: flowery shores,
and a procession, singing.

Stuck on this rock, mid-river,
I chant my mad song to no
enchanted sailors. Over and
over, my own words seal my ears.

Music Cruise

Coming at evening to the wet edge of the city,
we find the boat moored beside the dark
pilings, white as a shell, its string of lights
tacked up loosely to the sky. Down in the water,
jellyfish bloom and fold, hovering in a moth-dance;
wavetops tap along the hull and fall, like music.

They cast off; we find seats where the music
can reach us over the engines, and the city
is visible to starboard, just beyond the dance
of the cellist's fingers, picking notes out of the dark,
sleek hull of wood. The boat throbs into deeper water,
surprising the dull harbor with its noise and lights.

We had looked forward to a show of lights
from buildings at harborside, as we enjoyed the music
and sipped our wine, and glided lordly on the water.
Instead, they show us the heaped guts of the city:
track, slag and warehouse, everything ugly and dark.
The night falls flat; not even the wine will dance.

Why did we come here, believing the song-and-dance
in the radio ads, that promised us the lights
of stars and moon, the touch of summer breezes in the dark,
all but the smell of orchids, and tropic drums for music?
We could be dining on a high peak of the city,
smug, overlooking this slow, cold flow of water.

We can't even find the jellyfish under the water.
They might have amused us with their fragile dance,
but they flit like moths along the shallows near the city,
afraid of our wash, our blades, our garish lights.
They shun the crude chat and laughter that mar the music,
smudging the scrolls it traces on the dark.

At 8:00 sharp, the boat arrives at noplace in the dark
harbor and turns, spinning like driftwood on the water.
The night flips over: there's a new lilt in the music,
a young man and his sweetheart find room to dance,
and we gape, amazed by the sudden blaze of lights
stacked thick on the shore of a fabulous glass city.

Turned from the dark, we leave our wine and rise to dance
like moths above the water. We want only to glide beside
    these lights
through night after night of music, hymning the bright city.

III

Myths

A Winter's Tale

It's the stories I like best, and next best (though you
may think it's queer), the quiet. After all's been told,
for a time, and the new dead are settled, the hall's
so still I can hear Acheron chiming like bells
of glass—the sound that asphodels would make if they
could ring—out at the meadow's edge, under my white
poplars. There's no wind here; not anyplace on earth
could you find poplar leaves holding so still, as if
the next breath must bring sunrise, or a storm. Wanting
that moment, you will stand like stone—and nothing
will happen. The sun goes down daily into Ocean,
not into this realm. Nor does the moon, my sister,

visit. We do not count dark, light, dark, light, like girls
at a game of beads, or set a watch, like anxious
sailors, on the weather. What is to be is here;
the mind is free. Up there, everything's a scramble—
the girls go chatter chatter and my mother's
orders dance like bees around a hive: watch the lambs,
open the apple blossoms, see to the new wheat.
And in between, the spinning, the laundry, the tiles
to be scrubbed. No Olympian comforts—Mother's
not that sort. She's even hired out, I hear,
as a nursemaid lately in Eleusis. At home,
though, she commanded, as a goddess will, and let

Hades take anyone who shirked. Here, I am Queen.
They hailed me, those down along the shore, the moment
I came in sight. I was holding up my sheaf of wheat—

45

it seemed almost to light my way after the path
grew dark and steep. And one—a shade whose face I still
remember—looked up, and stopped his muttering, and said
to the next one, "The Queen." I thought he saw
some ghostly memory, but then he said my name,
"Persephone," as clear as day. "Persephone!
The Queen!" They crowded to the shore and hailed me,
"The Queen returns! Persephone returns!" The wheat
I held grew brighter; it flamed and then became

a sceptre in my hand. They said I had always
been the Queen here. And now it seems to me that's so,
although I recall that journey down the narrow
valley: the flowers, and then the rocky twilight—
how the wheat grew bright, and how my hounds took fright
and left me. I miss my hounds, but I am happy
here. I do no work but this fine weaving, as befits
a queen. It has a border of pomegranates
and snakes and in the cloth I weave shapes of women
and men—worked white on white, not easy to discern.
It is a web of stories, a cloth as endless

as the longings of the dead. I sit by this hearth
and listen—not to young girls' fuss and gossiping,
but to the shades of queens and warriors, sages,
murderers, lovers. Oh, the stories! My mother
would never let me sit there as long as I wished,
at the feet of any old crone who'd croon a tale.
Here I can listen till I've had my fill—the day
(or night) goes on forever, and the time to stop
the telling never comes. No one can say to me
"Get up, do this, do that." I am the one who says,
at last, "I've had enough. Let there be silence now."
They cannot be quiet forever, but they've learned
to wait. The Old Ones have the most to say—they take

turn after turn at talking, once for every life.
They are the only shades who come and go again,
weave back and forth between this hall and upper earth.
Prophetess, magician, healer, midwife, wild man,
witch—they have a trick they say the Phoenix teaches.
Listening, I have begun to learn it. The wheat
is like that, after all: dead in the ground, then grown
again. I will weave the secret into this web,
and hang it in the hall for all the dead to see.
This will displease my husband, him they call The Judge,
the Implacable One. He would keep them, heap them
here like riches in a cave. But I will sway him,

I will get my way. Hades is but a babe here;
I am Queen from the Beginning. The new dead say
they tell a tale on earth: a chariot, a rape,
another maiden gone. Hades enjoys this fame;
he won't disclaim it. But the shades remember this:
I came alone, on foot, holding a sheaf of wheat.
They hailed me, "She returns—the Queen." And when I saw
the flawless meadows, the streams like glass, the poplars
that seemed to hold their breath, I felt a queen's content.
It was a place where one could sit and think—except
for the muttering, the endless muffled jabber
of the dead. The dead cannot laugh or dance or mate,

but they can talk. "And then I hit him such a blow . . ."
"It was a lie! if I could . . ." "And me expecting
a baby any day . . ." Amazing! Every shade
was keeping his life in mind by babbling his tale.
And no one listened. Words bubbled up like water,
but no one drank, and none was satisfied. A queen
must rule, so when they changed to chanting out my name
I raised my voice and said, "You must be quiet, shades.
I want to hear the sound of no wind in the leaves,

the chime of asphodels. I want to trace the sound
of Acheron, like crystal bells, back to the spring
between the worlds. Then I will take you one by one

into my hall and hear you. I, Persephone,
will listen to your story, yes—and yours, and yours.
There will be time for everyone, there will be no
time. This will be my gift to you, and yours to me."
Then I lifted up my sceptre in the silence
and the sound of Acheron rang faint and fainter
back to the crack at earth's west edge. And since then,
I keep my promise—I sit and listen, I sit
and weave this web. The dead do not eat, or fuss
with fire and pots. And yet they feed me—a hunger
I have is filled. The fields of earth, I hear, are bare
now. Since I—who always did the most—am missing,

Mother lets everyone idle. Nothing need strive
to grow now, the streams are quiet ice, the ivy
is the only leaf. Unknowing, my Mother makes
the earth a place like this—for we are very much
alike, I must admit. Soon her realm will so approach
my own that I could visit—if I had my hounds,
I might go now. I'd like to see that world at rest,
no bustle of war or building. I'd course my hounds
across the white fields, perfect for retaining tracks,
and under the dreaming trees. I'd come to a hut,
a lodge, a castle, and I know what I would find
inside: a hearth, and mortals telling their stories.

On Her Fifteenth Birthday

"... she will not die, but sleep for a hundred years."

He's out of it already, old
fool slumped on the throne like a puppet someone's done with.
"A bonfire" (bright idea!)

"searches, a law against spindles!" No use, I told him,
but men have their ways—A to
B, nut to bolt, a sword or lock for every pickle.

My lord, that potentate, would make
his daughter safe or know the reason. He never knew
the reason, nor will the Prince—

scored red by thorns, gallumphing upstairs with his puissant
pucker—know that all he's done
is come, by chance, the day the curse runs out. A comet

could claim as much, credited
with birth and havoc. There's a time for everything—blood,
kisses, thorns, thrones —but they don't

grasp it. She does. She's at it already, counting down,
tick, tick. Dreaming a spindle
and a prick—a tower, rather, in the clouds, a horse,

a man with a sword. I know
the script, I've been there. Princess, Queen—I was the wicked
fairy, too, and the good ones,

49

the whole gold-plated dozen. I was the granny, crone
in the high cranny, spinning
the birthday toy she'd never laid an eye, a tiny

white hand on. I was the cook
and the chambermaids, I made the castle walls, courtyards,
stables. No labor that's not

my own—what pains I took to give that girl a life!
Now, in her dream-world, she sees:
it was Mother in all those masks! And in other, worse ones—

the one that dressed her in rags,
the one that ordered her heart brought back in a casket.
All those stories are hers now;

my work is done, and she's undoing it, wrapping up
her girlhood strand by strand, like
one who harvests cobwebs in a fairy tale. Dreaming,

she gathers, she understands.
She's got the Prince down pat, and the nap's just beginning.
Next comes the greater labor—

imagining a world she can wake up in. Make it
up she must, for no one else
has been there. Flying machines, glass towers, wizards that
    work

the weather, any other
wonder she comes up with. But everything must be covered—
governments, hedgehogs, jugglers—

details precise and slow as tapestry. Gradually,
on schedule, she'll get there:
stitch the last leaf as the Prince kneels, bleeding. Then the kiss,

the waking, etcetera,
like clockwork. She arrives, stale-breathed and dowdy
as any traveler, but

we will not. Weariness, now that she's gone, creeps heartward
from my feet. Flames, flowers, flies
in this castle may flicker up at spell's end, but not

the old bones on these two thrones.
Daddy chair and Mommy chair will sit here, waiting out
the date. We're not that patient,

can't stay put like stage props placed for the last act. Decay,
one might say, is a grace, more
natural than all this stasis. By the time she takes

the Prince around the place,
we will be back to basics—harmless horrors, mistakes
from another age. A grave,

a few words, whatever's decent, they'll decree before
leaving. Free, that's the main thing,
or so they'll think. Only a kink or two in the new

world, only a nightmare now
and then. Things seen in sleep—a King, a Queen. Old figures
from a tale: Fear, Anger, Grief.

Lost

On the familiar path above the pond, the known woods
ragged with leaf-fall, suddenly—that curve, that downed birch
on the far shore, you've never seen before. This forest,
halfway to winter, is new to you, substituted
who knows how? Confusion flattens it to tapestry:

black verticals, gilt ground. No pattern in this fabric
emerges to direct you left or right. A few steps,
guessing, and the woods round out again, separating
near from far. But where? A stranger, you keep the grey pond
in view and wander the redundancy of trunks. Oak,

pine, birch—the same, but named, now, in a different
   language.
You cannot rate the foreign gold that rustles under foot
and hangs still, piecemeal, on the trees. Your pockets, at any
rate, are empty: you have nothing to exchange. But strange
to say, you are not out of place. Safe passage you take

for granted; translation, even, teases at tongue-tip.
Not fish or fowl in the other world, here you could fit,
where possibility branches. There in the shallows,
whorls on a damp log transform to plumage where mallards
nap. That golden floor, mosaic of foliage, floats

on the pond top, tempting your foot's faith. Fallen needles
drift into deep beds (the color the Miller's daughter
spun), promising a hundred years of sleep. To keep watch,

citizens, staid and ancient, gather—here is a leaf,
pale tan, pored, and thin, that fits on your hand-back like skin.

Now the wind, in welcome, hurls gold handfuls, churns up earth
and sky. You might, it occurs, write just a word or two
on one bright scrap and send it flying back: "Do not weep,"
perhaps, or, to be plain, "Farewell." But now the litter
settles, the air is still. Sun's slant tells you there's little

time to find a place to root. Across the pond, grey branches
rise uphill and hang like smoke above a battlefield.
Soon you will learn the story of those forces: the King
dead without successor, the Tyrant toppled. High up,
unseen geese are trumpeting away. You cannot say,
yet, whether those notes announce retreat or victory.

Persephone to Hades, in Bed

Why did I let her go? I had no choice! I tried to mother
her with cushions and sweetmeats, but she wouldn't countenance
a comfort. Sat on the floor, ate common bread; showed the work
of some clever coach. But doubtless you saw it—you, the "Hidden
One," spied on that blasphemous beauty. Don't deny, husband,
you too have that drive to take a peek. Like this, see?

I lift the sheet, and—what divine magnificence I see!
Now, will you punish me? You know the Grief his mother
gave her—hopeless tasks, and Anxiety for her lost husband.
Hard on her looks, yes. Would you call that a countenance
to vie with Aphrodite? Still, should she have left him hidden—
obeyed, stayed tamely in that playland without rank or work?

Gods should know about these mortal females: forbidding
    them won't work.
She's aced every labor (with help—I sent the ants), and I'll see
her through the last one, bring to light that treasure hidden
in her belly. But isn't curiosity a gift! Even a mother-
to-be, exhausted, grieving, was keen to watch my countenance
for signs of envy when she described her palace and her husband.

Oh, like you. Light-shy, both old and young, a fabled husband
and evasive. A Wealthy One whose consort does no work
for Demeter, nor longs to be a girl again. That Lady's counte-
    nance
turned away, though Psyche begged her by my dark descent to
    see

54

the likeness. Decked like a bride—why?—I return to Mother
(as she does not), and all the summer keep my mourning
    hidden.

A life half light, half nighttime. She understands. What's hidden
is probably precious—no news to a girl whose husband
only shows up in the dark. The implications rub my mother
wrong, so our guest got nowhere with all her housework
in the temple. But she'll succeed, that peeker—she'll have to see
what's in the box. I put in Sleep, restorer of the countenance.

She wonders, in her dream, if that regretted countenance,
or Cupid's, or some stunning blend, is shaping in her hidden,
peek-proof casket! My envy of that is what she couldn't see—
How they go on, these mortals! I, invoked in childbed, give
    my husband
no child but myself—renewed here, then packed to the surface
    to work
myself old at Demeter's behest. You sleep, Lord, with your
    mother-

in-law, for I am my mother. It's my law bids you countenance
that girl's return from your hidden halls: they may never see
a birth. Her sleep's my work, and— Hark! the wingbeats of
    her husband!

The Mooncalf

Afternoon. The Great South Sea, just past
the Bashee Isles. The ship tranced in a tropic
        calm. On the masthead a young man dreams;
a sublime uneventfulness invests him.
        He scans the endlessly encircling
smooth blue. Those indolent, long swells, he thinks,
        are like a prairie stretching serene
beneath the sun. Tonight he will inscribe it
        in his notebook by whale oil light: "Stretched

serene, sunny, and . . ." Yes—*fecund* is the word
        to call that empty, tempting surface.
Cheek against the mast, he dreams it towering,
        taller, halfway to where the sun gleams
like a gold coin nailed onto the sky. Himself,
        colossal, parting the clouds with sper-
macetti perfumed hands, scans the Pacific,
        sees ships skate scattered like waterbugs
in their solitary stalking, crossing and

        crisscrossing the Line. "Look sharp, monkey!"
bellows a voice below. Awake, he cannot
        see the ships; he cannot see the whales'
submerged, converging paths, although he's noted
        that they travel now in packs. Thicker
than water, their spilled blood bonds new Armadas
        from the dwindling tribes. Or so he thinks—
in all his dreams there's nothing so fantastic
        as that wide net of clicks and crooning,

gossip and alarms flung farther than a dark,
 rope-thewed Tahitian arm could throw
the largest net that's drying down on the deck.
 Weightless, *diffused like Wickliff's sprinkled*
Pantheistic ashes, its coils elude him:
 he thinks those great fish (for fish he thinks
they are) go mute as men at sea, whose lanterns
 sign only to the eye, whose flags flap
crude news from mast to spyglass. He has not heard

 the lullabies. But once he saw them,
dams and their infants, a nursery of whales
 floating in the shadow of the ship,
suspended in clear depths. The young, while suckling,
 gazed away, as babies will, towards
some unearthly reminiscence, ignoring
 the ogling sailors as if they were
but a bit of Gulf-weed in their new-born
 sight. The mothers, lolled on their sides, seemed

quietly to eye the humans, mistrusting
 the truce. He dreams the scene again, lets
the maternal bulk below rock him to port,
 to starboard. He is the ship's boy, six
years old and black, leaned asleep against the mast
 between his legs. He hears the boy's voice—
his own voice!—piping, tiny in the huge blue
 air. He sings and strikes his tambourine;
the stretched Pacific pulses to his beat. Ah!

 Louder! Higher! He rides to the sky
like Jack on his exalted stalk. His giant
 song strides over the horizon, scrolls
an unfolding wind-rose on the globe. Jolted
 awake, eyes wide, hands grabbing balance,
he searches the empty sea. There, beneath

that flat shining that declares the sky
and nothing but the sky, the thing that he hunts
   is hiding. His heart—no, another,

an enormous, heart—is drumming, thundering
   up from the undiscoverable
bottom. Louder. Nearer. Now! The blunt brow bursts
   the surface, the shattered Pacific
glitters in the air. Inside that halo—whole,
   improbable, the creature hangs, flies,
writhes its comma on the sky. The young man breathes
   in, breathes out, without a sound. Below,
a shout goes up; the apparition plummets,

   piles up a mountain of dazzling foam.
Pulleys sing, boats hit the water, men over-
   board themselves and free-fall to their oars.
Out where the sperm-shape vanished, the brilliant mist
   falls dimming from the air. His name comes
up to him in frenzied cries. He shudders, slides
   like a bead to the gunwale and drops
to the boat. Late, berated, he pulls, curls, pulls
   with his mates. They will not make the kill,

his headsman snarls. The young man, indifferent—
   facing, as a rower will, away
from the goal—looks back to the ship, to the mast
   where it happened. He dreams a tiller
of whalebone and rows of barbaric teeth—new
   and *marvelous features, pertaining*
to the wild business. . . . The lead boat bays, "There she
   blows!" He will not speak all day, bemused
by the multitudinous unfolding: stout

Starbuck and dancing, demented Pip
and quilted Queequeg's god of generation.
The Bachelor, the Virgin, the Rose-
bud, the Delight. The Rachel mourning her lost
young. The *wild simultaneousness
of a thousand concreted perils.* Three days'
savage chase. *Swift vengeance, eternal*
malice, the huge, white, *predestinating head,*
and mad Ahab strangled by his cord.

IV

Riddles

Getting Clearer

Daily the forest is clearer
and you can see in farther
as fading foliage gets thinner.
Daily the passing jogger
labors a little harder,
for the mornings get colder
as you get closer to winter.

Reversing, the woods remember
March, when branches were barer
and skunk cabbage pierced the litter
of old leaves and needles. Better
go back and be naked, plainer
and blunter than ruffled summer.
Summer was always a riddler,

swaddler, muffler, deceiver,
hinting at what lay deeper,
remoter, ripe for the finder.
Now that the leaves are looser,
the view through the forest freer,
you see what you couldn't the other
days, before summer was over.

You see that the forest was never
hiding ulterior treasure
that only a hero could capture.
Anyone's eye can gather

that farther reflects the nearer:
tree behind tree getting grayer,
emptier, smaller, forever.

Only the greedy believer
supposed the oak leaves were cover
for charms to change the beholder.
Daily the forest is clearer.
Daily the passing jogger
looks through tree trunks harder,
wants to see farther, be surer.

Channel 2: Horowitz Playing Mozart

sits with a small smile, watching
two speckled frogs or lizards run right
and left, apart, together

on long legs bendable as rubber.
He doesn't bend down, looking,
or sway to keep up with their scuffles,

but sits immobile, his eyes
icon-sized but lidded, following
those mottled creatures. Bow-tied,

sweater-vested, he could be a clerk
at a counter, there to wrap
things up for us the old-fashioned way,

with brown paper and a string.
He is old, no doubting it; his lean
head states the skull's theme clearly.

Strict time has taught him patience, practice
this perfect stillness, amused,
a little, like Buddha, watching two

lithe, spotted beasts (allegro)
in their hopscotch hurry. Now stealthy
(lento), now frantic, they ramble

and attack and he observes, as if
to learn their motives—hunger?
fear? territorial contention?

They could be hoarding, like ants,
against the future, or this display
might be, in fact, a mating

dance (as we, the viewers, are hoping
in our hearts). They are not tame,
exactly, or exactly trapped—that

man is kindly, it strikes us,
and would release them. He is admiring,
it seems, the precision, worked

out in all this time—the way they fit
their niche. Just the parts they need
they have evolved: the long and recurved

reachers, the last joints padded
hammer heads. He glances now and then
at Previn, the beat-keeper.

"They will go on forever,"
he might be saying, "unless your stick
can make an end of it." There —

the cut-off falls, the last chord
lingers in the strings. The old man flings
them—winged?—up into the air,

a referee (that bow tie)
declaring both the winner, sending
them heavenward, letting go.

Ciphers

No one exclaims at these perfect circles
appearing without aid of stencil

or compass everywhere—in cisterns,
ponds, bathtubs, glasses of Perrier, Lake

George, gutters. The ocean, were it calm
enough, would grow moon-faced with a rash

of rings begun with a "plip" and swift
in their growth as a breath—one intake,

strangely, just the time it takes a ridge
of water to expand its exact

circumference (barring collision's
interference) to the pre-set

point of vanishing. Erased, replaced
by the next concentric, or wrinkling

through miracles of intersection,
one equation, writ insistently

in water, contradicting the tall,
cool glass, the taxicabs, the hemlocks

around the pond. As if to be wheeled,
rigid, leafy, breathing, were a mere

doily on the law behind it all.
Or out front, rather—on the asphalt,

the swimming pool, the pasta pot. Shards
everywhere you look, pocked with the same

unnatural perfection, smoothing
themselves on the intake of a breath

shaped in no "oh" of admiration
and never let out in dread. Not one

of us exclaims, hiding in health clubs,
offices, behind the trees, our insides

sloping toward the moon, our wet brains ticking
output—"concentric," "circumference,"

ringed in imperfect bone and waiting
till nightfall to venture down to drink.

Thanksgiving

The trees have recovered, it seems, from their seizure
of fevered leaves. The woods are calm now, gray and staid

brown, like the Pilgrims we used to cut from paper.
Walk with me under the emptied oaks and the gray

sky, creased by geese in their long V's, leaving. Nothing
here is bright but a bunch of berries, red, set off

by the leafless branch, the gray woods, the afterdrops
of rain that varnish the red cluster, then fatten

into beads and fall. Walk with me, for I am tired
of the same old combination: myself walking

in Nature (more than forty years now), a little
puzzle in a Mystery. Come play your part, you,

twenty-one years my partner. Bring your brain, that bright
learner; indulge my explanations. "Think," I'll say,

"how all this—the emptying, the ending—is like
a costume change, a new stage in the entertainment.

There are impoverished places with nothing but green
leaves, ever. This depletion is our increase, seen

aright. Moreover, there's another season still,
if you can credit it, all white and shining."

And further to sway you, I will offer gifts: "See,
the red berries, the arrowhead of geese. Come here,

to the pond's edge, where mud is whitening to lace.
In a week we will be walking on the water."

Also, in winter

one must have a body,
warm and fed and glassed in,
to regard the capillaried oaks

dividing on the sky
and netting the white ground
with neural shadows—weightless,

accurate, stretched from the trunk
at changing angles: anticipation,
presence, memory—and think

of the deltas seaweed makes
between the drift of dunes
and the breakers' white accumulations;

or of the hooked fish that so resembled
that last leaf, wind-jerked
and struggling on the bough.

One must have been inside a while
to think about the mind:
how it can be convinced for a time

that it is nothing itself
(a sheet of glass, of ice)
and pass, in that instant,

a plenitude—what is there, and what
is not—to the beholder,
warm in her fed body.

Presbyopia

Old eyes, but wiser, says the Greek. You lose sight of guide-
    lines: I before E, Every Good Boy
    Does Fine, Insert Tab A in Slot B.
Things arrive, at this late date, unlabelled. All that book-

    learning a waste now—even your mate,
at close range, blurs, becomes a surface with a taste.
Unlettered, you take up jungle tactics, sniff and grope.
    You might regress to tom-toms, but who

would answer? Puzzles crowd your path like carnivorous
    plants; your hand goes crazy, writing checks
    to New England Telepath and Faust
National Bunk. Your grocery list asks for the "apple

    of life," then "ravishes, letups, grace."
A meaning leans in with a wink—a wing-beat and it's
off into the mist. Is a message mixed with all this
    mystery—advice from the next life

for folks who are losing their focus on this one?
    Is your own hand the medium, patched
    in to paradise, scribe for Something
Higher? If so, is it advisable to heed it—

    "fix radiances, take out paupers"?
Not likely, after the time spent getting sensible.
Even uncoded, the Word will turn out some old saw,
    no doubt: "Love thy neighbor," or "Buy low,

sell high." You'll try to apply it, but it won't win
        any prize. Suppose, though, there's a clue
        in the works, something useful. Like, "You
there, heads up! Nothing on paper can save you! Watch that

        horizon, out where the sea might be."
A tip to heed, if that's the reading. Indeed, you've had
suspicions—glimpses of something gallumphing there, whiffs
        of the foul or fishy, creeping up

the beach. You can almost see it now, like a squid, but
        bigger. Keep an eye out, while there's time
        to imagine alternatives. Keep
reading the signs: "Deaf End," "Private Poverty," "Wet Pain . . ."

V

The Land of Milk and Honey

The Land of Milk and Honey

"Keep to the West, where the sun sets, and you cannot
fail to find her."
L. Frank Baum, *The Wonderful Wizard of Oz*

I. Bedford, Massachusetts. September, 1994.

September, and heat hangs on. The late rose drops
        a spotted petal; border beds grow leggy
                and transgress. Trees tarnish—the first few

loose leaves loop-the-loop past bees that reel
        in bacchanal where blue grapes
                burst and shrivel. The apple

trees, disorderly,
        drop random apples
                like picnickers littering

the grass. It's gone for good, that
        golden age, that myth, that period
                of ordered fruitfulness. Now crows crowd

the yard with their dark omens; loud skeins of geese
        are leaving, and in the night I understand
                their cries. Give me my curious staff,

my stubborn boots, my scrip of learning,
        and I too, disorderly,
                bleeding/not bleeding without

rhyme or reason, will
    forsake the garden
        and take my pilgrimage. Not

south with the flying migrants
    or east into the sea or north where
        death holds court. I will go widder-

shins, against earth's turning, like those old women
    who danced naked in the woods while farmers scythed
        beneath the harvest moon. The Only

Child is waiting, and She whose garden
    grows gold roses contrary
        to the snow. I'll bundle what's

needed—bread, kettle,
    matches, cheese, tampons—
        in this old patchwork the great-

great-great-aunts made. The moon,
    who changes and forgives the fickle,
        will glide through the night the way that I

am going. Give me two apples from the grass-
    red for blood, gold for a token—and I'll flit
        like a gypsy levering the latch.

II. Mt. Carroll, Illinois. April, 1843.

My very dear Mother: I thank God
we are safe arrived and all in health.
Abram is like a young lamb "skipping
upon the hills" after so long pent

up on flatboat and steamer. Will works
like an ox to start his farm and sees
the golden fields, like El Dorado,
in his dreams. Your rose has been planted!
It rode wrapped in burlap, well propped

between the churn and the pineapple
bedstead. Now it commences its new
life, under the south-facing window
where I sit to send word to my Dear
Ones. You would not credit how quickly
a house can rise here with the labor
of a score of neighbors. Sorely as we
miss you all and our old home, we've come,
I believe, into that land of milk

and honey that pilgrims are vouchsafed
in the wilderness. Our new friends gave
us beds and fed us (was it just ten
days ago?) and then, like the genie
in the tale you used to tell, they made
us, overnight, this dwelling. No halls
of gold, it's true, but here's my dear old
escritoire and Aunt Davina's chest
of drawers, and the pineapple bedstead

filling half the space! Will promises
a big brick house within the year—I
say "We'll see" to that and thank the Lord
for a house that doesn't rock. You know,
Mother, that the Indians moved West
from here in 1804; there are some
few left, who roam the land like gypsies.
They are sharp dealers, stealers of eggs
and chickens, but otherwise nothing

to fear. Some of the women sell charms
and simples and have skill in healing.
One such, a midwife, proved of great help—
not here, but back on the Ohio,
at a place called Shawneetown, when young
Jane Beckwith (whose husband, you'll recall,
shared with Will the purchase of the boat)
was taken beforetimes with her pains.
The boathands swore at us, the husband

cried, I grasped Jane's hand and bathed her brow—
and Abram watching in that one-room
flatboat shanty! We made Shawneetown
at midnight. No doctor, but they sent
for Squaw Susannah, who dosed poor Jane
with a brew of willow twigs and made
her squat to help the baby's coming.
I knelt behind and held her and felt
her labor almost as my own. Oh,

Mother, the anguish! Without the aid
of that woman from the woods, I think
we would have perished—Jane, the baby,
and myself from pity. But young Pearl
squalled and guzzled like Gargantua,
though she looked like one of Calico's
runts. We laid them on clean straw,
with our best quilts for a cover,
for the fire outside on the sandbox

was our only heat. The squaw went off
with a dollar in silver coin—poor
thanks, but all she'd take. Will calls Pearl our
Cleopatra, who arrived by barge,
and Pearl laughs as if she sees the joke.

But I thought more of Mary, the young
mother, as Jane sat wrapped by the fire
and gave suck while Bess our cow and Guy
the mule and Clancy the plough horse hung

their gentle heads over her shoulders.
As we went on, the trees on either
hand began to bud. At Cairo, where
we met the Mississippi, a mist
of new green filled the forest. Then north
by steamer, and the spring came with us.
At St. Louis we saw two hundred
Wyandots debarking with their poor
possessions, headed west to Kansas,

where I pray they will find a good life.
Now Pearl is stirring here beside me,
and I must call Jane in to feed her—
Jane works like a man while I idle,
for Mother, Abram's little sister
(so I hope) will be here by summer's
end! How I will miss you when my time
arrives! In this strange place, familiar
things give me courage—the old bedstead

where you lay to bear me, the cradle,
the quilts, the rose. But I must close. Pearl's
cries pierce my bosom, and she must have
her mother! Give Father and Mabel
a kiss for me, and my love to all
the Dear Ones, and do plan a visit
to us, it is quite safe by steamer
or by stage. From Anna B. Graham
to her Mother, Susan H. Bowman.

III. Hollywood, Illinois. July, 1923.

Love me   or I will die
    his dark eyes bur-   ning into mine.
        The handsome Sheik   creeps in my tent,
            the blood-red rose   to tell his love . . .

                Oh, God, Mama's telling it
again—the rose on the flatboat floating down
the damn Ohio. I could say that out loud—
"the damn Ohio." But not here, in Mama's

garden—I'll say it to Frankie when I see
him, "Mama was telling the Indin woman
about her old rose bush coming down the damn
Ohio." Why should the Indin woman care?

She only wants Mama to buy that dumb dried-out
twist of weeds, like a chicken's foot. Her hand looks
like a chicken's foot, the Indin, the old witch.
She told Mama her mother was a gypsy,

her father was an Indin chief. They all lie—
but she could be a gypsy, those golden hoops,
that rag around her head. She might have danced, once,
around the fire, while men watched with burning eyes.

    Flaming
        with all the glow of   sunrise
            a burning kiss is   sealing
                the vow that all be - tray.

        For the passions that   fill love
            and lift you high to   heaven
                are the passions that   kill love
                    and let you fall to   hell . . .

Mama should say she kills a chicken every
Sunday and the blood feeds the roots of the rose.
That's the way gypsies talk, but Mama's so dull—
All she said was, "You've come sick now; it happens

every month." She should have said, "You're a woman
now, a full-blown rose." It's not just the bleeding
and the rag box—it's getting breasts and dancing
in the moonlight and fellows loving you so

they want to die. I might have to run away
if things don't change, across the Mississippi
to where the real Indins live. My hair is dark
like theirs, I can dance a gypsy dance and make

potions to drive men mad. I'll have the second
sight, the way that woman knows I have the curse.
"Good for the change," she tells Mama, and she waves
the weed thing like a wand.

     when I'm calling you-oo-oo-oo-oo-oo-oo
         will you answer too-oo-oo-oo-oo-oo-oo?

        That means I   offer my love to
          you   to be your own

         If you re-   fuse me, I will be
            blue   and waiting all alone

          Mama'd be happy
forever in her damn garden. She looks like
an old woman already, gray hair falling
down out of its pins. "Cross my palm with silver,"
says the Indin. Mama turns her back to me

and pays. I won't sleep tonight in the old bed
that came down the damn Ohio, where Mama's
Mama was born. I'll climb out the window, down
the apple tree, and dance in the moonlight, dance

with a rose in my teeth. Out there, westward through
the trees, I'll see the campfires flicker and I'll
run. Beyond the great river, under the moon,
I'll dance for my brave, my wild copper lover.

And then—ah, then!—out of the fiery sunset,
Tom Mix on his golden palomino comes
thundering and they struggle in the dust and one
will die for me. For me! for he loves me so.

I'll be the Rose   of Istamboul
          up on the screen   in every town

          my flashing eyes   will drive them wild
                    when Frankie sees   he'll want to die

          when Mama sees   she'll understand
                    she never knew . . .
                    she never knew . . .

Yes, Mama, I made my bed and fed the cat
and dusted. Yes, I'll go start the kettle, like
a girl in a nursery rhyme. Mama, you don't
know about a thing except your damn old rose.

IV. Hollywood, Illinois. May, 1950.

Dorothy was an orphan. I don't know
          why they died, it doesn't say.
She loved Aunt Em, though, and they all came
          to live in Oz finally—Aunt

Em and Uncle Henry and Toto.
        They stayed in the Emerald
Palace (real emerald, not pretend,

        like with the Wizards' glasses)
and Dorothy was a Princess. In Oz,
        nobody changes—babies
don't grow up, ever, and nobody
        dies. I'd never have to lie
down with a hot pad and wear Kotex
        things like my sister. I wish

we could live there and be happy—my
        mother, daddy, my sister
and even my brother. He couldn't
        pick on a Princess of Oz
who's Dorothy's best friend. And Ozma's too—
        she has a television
that shows what's going on in every

        part of Oz—Munchkin country
in the East, where Dorothy started from,
        and the Winkies in the West,
and the Quadlings and the Gillikins.
        I can read the book myself.
At bedtime, I pretend my mother's
        reading to me. Her kiss-mark

shines on my forehead like fireflies
        after I turn off the light.
She got very bad and had to go
        away. But she's only sick,
not dead, like Dorothy's mother. She'll come
        back, the way Glinda came back
in that giant bubble, and dance her

gypsy dance in the kitchen.
Nobody gets sick in Oz, or mad
       or nasty, and no fighting
is allowed. People will let you sleep
       in their houses if you just
knock at the door. You don't need money;
       sandwiches and cookies grow

on trees. Dorothy has satin dresses
       and silver shoes—not ruby
slippers, they changed that in the movie.
       She took them right off the feet
of the dead witch and they fit. She killed
       both bad witches, only not
on purpose. When people said "You must

       be a mighty sorceress,"
she'd say, "I'm only a little girl"
       and ask if they knew the way
to Kansas. I'd stay in Oz. There are
       some bad kinds of people there,
like Nomes and Hammer-Heads, but Ozma's
       trying all the time to make

them good or push them to the edges,
       out by the Deadly Desert.
Ozma's a little girl, but she's Queen,
       and nobody can boss her.
Dorothy never has to work. Except
       once, when the bad witch made her
a slave, before Dorothy learned to use

       her power. The silver shoes
could bring my mother home, if I could
       send them to her. Then we might

move to California. That's like Oz,
    full of flowers and singing
and all in Technicolor. The shoes
    always had the power, but

Dorothy didn't know it. So no one
    can blame her, and not even
Ozma could bring Dorothy's real mother
    back. Nothing was Dorothy's fault
at all—that cyclone just picked the house
    up and dropped it. And besides,
Dorothy was only a little girl.

V. Carlsbad, California. February, 1995.

Sitting in air, like that witch Miss Gulch in her rocking
    chair, I nap my way across the patch-
        work map. Lunch over Denver,
        then the movie. The deadly
    desert reels out below, unseen. No
pilot drones, "On the right, the Chocolate Mountains," or notes

that we're over the Old Woman range. The metal house
    descends past Havasu, Shoshone,
        Tecopa, and Antelope
        Center. We land at LAX light
    as a bubble and then I'm hugging
the Only Child and she is home again, zoomed to my

cuddling by the carousel. Her dark hair is hennaed;
    the happy ending sunshine lights up
        six silver piercings in one
        comely ear. Her jacket's black
    leather, her jeans are called Cherokee.
She drives like an ace; we follow the quick road slowly

south among the thousand thousand pilgrims conveying
        their petitions down the coast. Our quest
                ends at the Hacienda
                del Sol, a home for golden
        agers. On my mother's door a page
torn from *Newsweek* proclaims in large letters that "The Rules

Have Changed." She fits in my embrace a little strangely,
        growing smaller every year. She peers hard
                at her daughter's daughter's face
                like an old priestess scrying
        augeries. "You look like my mother,"
she declares, "and like your father, some, and like a wild

Indin, and like Michael Jackson." She grasps the girl through
        all these changes, to make sure she ends
                up ours. "Chill, Grandma." A pout,
                pretending. "You're such a pain."
        The ritual finished, we enter
with our bags and ask about the sign stuck on her door.

"Well," she says, still the sybil, "you know that the rules *have*
        changed." And that's that. Out in the garden
                we greet the naked cherub
                who stood once in our back yard
        in Illinois. "She's very happy
here," Mother confides. "And so am I—it's like living

in the Garden of Eden." "Funny you should say that,
        Mom." I steal her sentence, stow it whole
                in my pocket. "Our gardeners
                aren't too bad," she says, as if
        they were deaf. "They're Mexican, you know."
"Grandma!" But the gardeners smile, knowing (we hope) that old

ladies have their ways. We admire the dahlias, the birds
     of paradise, the tiger lilies,
          and the roses, none of which
          descended the Ohio
     in a flatboat. Now we're out the gate
and down the steep steps, single file, to the Pacific's

seething edge. The youngest runs down into the pounding
     rhythm and the ancient, salty scent
          of generation. We two
          old ones descend more slowly,
     knowing the ocean can wait. The waves,
an unlikely, indisputable blue, bear surfers

boogying on down to shore. My daughter dances back
     to meet us and walks with her Grandma,
          talking about Life. "These guys
          I live with . . . well, three . . . but only one
     I like . . . no, L.A.'s fine at night, but
funky, you know . . ." Grandma bestows her blessing: "I think

I'll just send you a gun and a box of condoms." She's
     right—the rules have changed. E.g., the sun
          sinking into the ocean
          like a reddened fruit instead
     of rising from it. And in the east,
the mountains release a moon-white egg and Eden comes

around again at the farthest edge of what might be
     a dream. "And you were there, and you, and
          you." The Only Child leans back
          into my arms and I lean
     back in my mother's, home again. Rocking,
we watch the west for omens unfolding in the gold.

The James Dickey Contemporary Poetry Series
Edited by Richard Howard

The Land of Milk and Honey
Sarah Getty

All Clear
Robert Hahn

Traveling in Notions
The Stories of Gordon Penn
Michael J. Rosen

United Artists
S. X. Rosenstock